# A Couple of
# Blaguards

# A Couple of Blaguards

*A Play*
*by Malachy & Frank McCourt*

Welcome Rain Publishers
NEW YORK

This Welcome Rain edition: May 2013
10  9  8  7  6  5  4  3  2  1
Printed and bound in the United States of America
ISBN 10: 1-56649-961-5
ISBN 13: 978-1-56649-961-3

# INTRODUCTION
*by Malachy McCourt*

It all began at a party in the living room of Brian and Sheila Brown when my brother Frank McCourt suggested we get up and play the characters who lived in our slum in the dreary town of Limerick, Ireland.

In most places in our world, lack of formal education inhibits colorful speech, but let me assure you that in Limerick that was not the case. When the King of England Henry II got permission from Pope Adrian IV to invade Ireland in the year 1169, and thereafter tried to ram his culture, his language, his philosophy, and his tyranny down the gullets of the Irish, he did not realize that one day they would take his language and elevate it to heights never envisioned by any Brit. As one critic said, "The Irish derive the greatest benefit from the English language: they court it like a beautiful woman, they make it bray with donkey laughter, they fling it at the sky like paint pots full of rainbow colours"...and that's what the McCourts heard in the slums of Limerick.

There were toothless women flinging their black fringed shawls about their shoulders like matadors, as they faced each other in verbal combat a hundred yards apart, rectifying perhaps an insult that had been offered one of the children. Case in point, here's a typical exchange between two antagonists.

**FIRST WOMAN:** "There are some in this lane who claim their husband was wounded in the war. Wounded he was, and he running from the enemy and the backs of his legs being penetrated by his own hard balls of shit."

**SECOND WOMAN:** "And there are some in this lane who have twin daughters and Irish names are not good enough for them. O NOOO, they had to name them after what they thought were two Italian saints, Syphilis and Gonorrhea."

And there were stick-wielding teachers, doomsday priests, and dopey politicians. One of the latter gave more tortuous and hilarious speeches than were ever delivered by Dan Quayle or George Bush. He promised to put shoes on all the poor footless children of Limerick, and he offered to build public lavatories the length and breadth of the town and they would have urinals for the man and arsenals for the woman.

America fulfilled all our dreams. Yes there were naysayers and alarmists amongst the Irish who had been here a long time and had lost their sense of decency of history and had become brain damaged by embracing conservatism, thereby fulfilling the Irish poet's prophecy: "You eventually become the thing you hate the most." But it was here in America I was able to wade into any field of endeavor that did not require professional training. So, I became a bar owner, an actor, a television talk-show host (ditto on radio), a gubernatorial candidate in New York, a columnist, and author of the bestseller *A Monk Swimming* and seven other books, and, of course, this play *A Couple of Blaguards*.

Additionally, I found the love of my life, Diana, who taught me how to say "I love you" in a meaningful, uninhibited way, and for almost the half a century that we have been married that's the loving way it has been.

Frank had his love of learning fully satisfied when by some subterfuge he was able to conceal his lack of high school qualifications and got admitted to New York University. He became the beloved teacher of thousands, and, eventually, after years of encouraging young students to write their stories, he put his own autobiography down on paper, and that story garnered awards and worldwide acclaim, including the Pulitzer Prize.

On the personal level, he was bedeviled by a disastrous marriage that lasted too long. Then he met a sunny, optimistic young woman, Ellen, with whom he was happy and who cheered him on and made sure he was able to sit down and write and finally produce his classic memoir, the book named *Angela's Ashes*.

*A Couple of Blaguards* is a light-hearted account of life in our slum and of our early lives in America, salted with oddly jolly descriptions of death, disease, and despair. Since it preceded our books, it could be regarded as a distant springboard, but it is no way *Angela's Ashes*.

Very loosely, it is meant to convey a bit of drama, a lot of comedy, and a few tears but, most importantly, it is intended for people who want to lose weight because we have high hopes that you will laugh your arse off and finish reading with a smile on your lips and a song in your heart.

If you are not of Celtic stock, 'tis unlikely you will be able to divine the meaning of the term "blaguards." It is, in fact, a corruption of the words "black guard," and black guards were legendary dockworkers who specialized in unloading coal from English ships in the harbor of Dublin.

As the day waned, the lads rendezvoused at their favorite pubs, still clad in blackened work clothes as well as blackened skins. Being through with their manual labor freed them to give vent to hi-jinks, roughhousing, singing, and whooping it up of every variety. Some of them had to make sure there was no pilferage from the ship, so they became known as "guards"—inevitably, "black guards."

A popular legend has it that the venerable Dean of St. Patrick's, Jonathan Swift, bestowed the moniker on our rowdy lads. Consequently, blaguards evolved into an affectionate name for youngsters misbehaving, being naughty, or just acting up.

Growing up Catholic in Ireland was indistinguishable from growing up breathing. Nobody was safe from Holy Mother Church, as her tentacles spread everywhere. All over were her priests, roaring, exhorting, counseling, baptizing, marrying, blessing, punishing, and importuning.

Whilst the image of the church was female, it was both sacrilegious and blasphemous to suggest that a woman become a priest. She was perfect enough to bear the body and blood of Jesus Christ, but inadequate to celebrate the mass.

Another loony practice required couples to go to be counseled by a celibate priest, who was prohibited from holding a woman in his arms and loving her. One of the most absurd incidents in the annals of the McCourts, related in *Blaguards,* was the day of Frank's First Communion. (You don't have to be Catholic to enjoy this one!)

In the Second Act, Frank's great story involving his care (or lack of same) of a few dozen canaries will have you holding your sides (bird lovers might not applaud this misadventure).

There is a British tradition of smilingly issuing a pejorative aside when speaking of the Irish. They, the Brits, regard us as if we were a mob of unruly children who shout, babble, and engage in extremely rough, sometimes dangerous and fatal play. We are, therefore, an irresponsible lot, separate from the human race, who must be disciplined at frequent intervals. Most of the so-called aristocratic elites of England are of Teutonic (mostly Prussian) descent, and consequently devoid of humor, playfulness, mythology, and imagination.

The Irish, being oppressed by a foreign church, having suffered subsequent invasions by Vikings, Normans, and English, had to revert to the spoken word, and with imaginations untrammeled by the strictures of respectability, organized religion, or proper grammar, they let fly with torrents of words, poetic, wild, natural, and joyous, leading the academic Brits to dismiss Irish language skills as "kissing the Blarney Stone," or "having the gift of the gab," but never are they praised for their eloquence.

Before the advent of written language, the histories and sagas of mankind were preserved by storytellers (called "seanachies" in Ireland). Due to British oppression, the Irish were forbidden under pain of death to print anything or even speak in Irish. Consequently, they spoke and sang in code and elevated English from a flat Teutonic soundscape into a colorful, wild flowering stream of torrential energy, overwhelming their slave masters with the power of the word.

*A Couple of Blaguards* is a compilation of stories of death, disease, and despair, assembled to ensure laughter at what was acknowledged to be a miserable life, for not alone the McCourt family, but for hundreds of thousands of others throughout Ireland.

# A Couple of
# Blaguards

## CHARACTERS

FRANK
MALACHY

## SETTING

Anywhere. Kitchen.

## SONGS

*Limerick is Beautiful*
*Barefoot Days*
*Confraternity Men to the Fight*
*There's No One With Endurance Like the Man Who Sells Insurance*
*Three Lovely Lasses from Limerick* (based on *Two Lovely Lasses from Bannion*)
*The Irish Rover*
*Some Say the Devil's Dead*
*There's a Big Ship Sailing on the Illy Ally Oh*
*A Mother's Love is a Blessing*
*Celeste Aida*
*Goodbye Muirsheen Durkin*
*Goodbye Johnny Dear*
*Yankee Doodle Dandy*
*I Don't Work for a Living*
*Bells of Hell*

*(FRANK and MALACHY enter. They pour drinks. They toast each other and the audience.)*

**MALACHY.** Frank!

**FRANK.** Malachy!

**BOTH.** *(to audience)* ...and your noble selves.

**FRANK.** I'm from Limerick.

**MALACHY.** So am I!

**FRANK.** Limerick is oldest city in Ireland. Second oldest in the British isles. It sits where the river Shannon swings to the right and emigrates to America for itself.

**MALACHY.** Limerick is a very ancient city with walls, ruins, and crumbling castles. It's so historic the favorite word of the Limerickman is 'was.'

**FRANK.** And the women of Limerick! Oh. The women. Is there anyone in the civilized world who hasn't heard of their beauty. Their piety and the ferocity of their chastity? The favorite word of the Limerick woman is 'no.'

**BOTH.** *(alternating)*

City of churches and beautiful spires.

City of pubs and of lowly desires.

City of gossips that wait to be told.

City of youth that wait to grow old.

Society's city. Home of the snob.

Show me your penny before you hobnob.

Do have a coffee do have a bun.

Do what the others do cause it is done.

**MALACHY.** Limerick is a handsome city with broad streets. Flanked by elegant Georgian houses. We did not live in an elegant Georgian house: we lived in a lane and not ten feet from our kitchen there was a slimy gutter oozing down the middle.

**FRANK.** It's a great misfortune to live in a Limerick lane. In the grand scheme of things the lane is barely above the poor house. For if you live in a lane...

**MALACHY.** You're poor.

**FRANK.** You live on bread and tea.

**MALACHY.** You have a flat accent.

**FRANK.** You wipe your snotty nose on your sleeve.

**MALACHY.** Your arse hangs out of the hole in your trousers.

**FRANK.** Your mother patches the hole...

**MALACHY.** And patches the patches...

**FRANK.** Till there's nothing left of the original trousers.

**MALACHY.** If you live long enough you'll leave school at the age of fourteen and get a job as a messenger boy.

**FRANK.** But your great dream is to get out of the lane altogether, and you might someday because your mother has a cousin in a place called

**BOTH.** Brooklyn.

**MALACHY.** Desperate suffering we had.

**FRANK.** Classic, I'd say.

**MALACHY.** And we've tried to forget, haven't we? We've tried...

**FRANK.** Religion

**MALACHY.** Education

**FRANK.** Emigration

**MALACHY.** Assimilation

**FRANK.** Sophistication

**MALACHY.** Masturbation

**FRANK.** Fornication

**MALACHY.** And it all comes back to Limerick.

**FRANK.** And the father.

**MALACHY.** Ah. The father. He came from the North of Ireland. So he did. And he sang. So he did.

**FRANK.** And he got the Irish divorce. So he did.

MALACHY. What is the Irish divorce, Frank?

FRANK. He disappeared. So he did.

MALACHY. And there we were, poverty-stricken, destitute, the poor mother not knowing what to do. Ah, the poor Mother.

FRANK. *(sings)*
SURE I LOVE THE DEAR SILVER THAT SHINES IN YOUR HAIR,
AND THE BROW THAT'S ALL FURROWED AND WRINKLED
   WITH CARE.
I KISS THE DEAR FINGERS SO TOIL-WORN FOR ME.
OH, GOD BLESS YOU AND KEEP YOU, MOTHER MACHREE.

MALACHY. Mother Machree, my arse.

FRANK. Mother Church.

MALACHY. Mother Ireland.

FRANK. Like all Irishmen, we were trapped in a trinity of maternities.

MALACHY. Oh, the miserable childhood.

FRANK. Oh, the sorrow and the suffering.

MALACHY. Not to mention the suffering and the sorrow.

FRANK. Ochone, ochone, and woe is me.

MALACHY. Musha, musha, musha...

FRANK. Wirra, wirra, wirra.

MALACHY. What are we to do with the miserable childhood?

BOTH. Ochone, ochone, ochone, and woe is me.
   *(both springing up)*
   *(sing)*
BAREFOOT DAYS, OH BOYS, THE THINGS WE DID.
WE'D GO DOWN TO A SHADY OLD NOOK,
AND WITH A BENT PIN FOR A HOOK
WE'D FISH ALL DAY, FISH ALL NIGHT
BUT THE DARNED OLD FISH REFUSED TO BITE.
AND THEN WE'D SLIDE DOWN SOME OLD CELLAR DOOR
BO DE OH DE OH, SLIDE AND SLIDE

TILL OUR PANTS GOT TORE.
THEN WE'D HAVE TO GO HOME STAY IN OUR BED, TILL
   MOTHER GOT BUSY WITH THE NEEDLE AND THREAD.
OH, BOY, WHAT JOY WE HAD IN BAREFOOT DAYS.
BOE-DEE-OH-DEE-OH-DOH
*(sit)*

**FRANK.** With all our suffering and all our sorrows we had a consolation, the One, Holy, Roman, Catholic, and Apostolic Church.

**MALACHY.** And weren't we lucky to live in the holiest city in Ireland?

**FRANK.** Weren't we fortunate we were never far from a church and the sound of the bells? The Angelus morning, noon and night: Mass at dawn, Benediction at dusk, Novenas, Retreats and the Stations of the Cross.

**MALACHY.** The parish bells: byong byong, byong byong, byong byong.

**FRANK.** The Convent bells: ting ting, ting ting, ting ting.

**MALACHY.** And the Protestant bells: Oh, I say there, Bong.

**FRANK.** And the bells of the great priestly orders: The Augustinians:

**MALACHY.** Bong Bong.

**FRANK.** The Fransicans:

**MALACHY.** Bong Bong.

**FRANK.** The Jesuits:

**BOTH.** WHAM!

**FRANK.** And above all the Redemptorists:

*(both stand)*

**BOTH.** *(pulling on an imaginary bell rope)* BONG BONG, BONG BONG, BONG BONG!

**MALACHY.** Bells with balls.

**FRANK.** The bells that called us of the archconfraternity of the Holy Family, the largest sodality in the world with its own marching hymn.

**BOTH.** *(march and sing)*
CONFRATERNITY MEN TO THE FIGHT
RAISE UP YOUR BANNERS ON HIGH
JESUS, MARY AND JOSEPH IN SIGHT
IN OUR BATTLES THEIR NAMES BE OUR CRY

**FRANK.** And every year at the retreat there was a sermon by a Redemptorist priest imported from the North of Ireland.

**MALACHY.** *(as preist)* We will begin by renewing our Baptismal vows. Do ye promise to renounce the Devil and all his works and wiles and pomps?

**FRANK.** We do.

**MALACHY.** I can't hear ye! Let your voices reverberate through the caverns of Hell and let Satan know he is in peril. Once more. Do ye renounce the Devil and all his works and wiles and pomps?

**FRANK.** We do, the dirty bastard

**MALACHY.** Much better. In the name of the Father, of the Son and of the Holy Ghost, Amen. Ah, my dear boys, I'm so glad to see so many of you at this retreat. How pleased our blessed Lord must be and his most pure mother, the purest of the pure... Is there a more precious possession than a pure soul? If you lose your soul, what do you have? Nothing. Let us reflect, then, on those two boys who, last year, instead of coming to the retreat went swimming, swimming they went in the river Shannon and without bathing suits... Heedless of their naked state they cavorted in sinful glee until in one awful moment they were caught in a crosscurrent, swept away and drowned. Drowned they were. Did they have a moment to repent? No. Did they have a moment to say an act of contrition? No. Did they have a moment to ask God's forgiveness? No. Where are they tonight? Down below with his satanic majesty, their souls plucked from their naked shriveled bodies and cast into the fiery flames of hell. Oh, the eternal torment. Oh, the burning. Oh, the scorching, the sizzling intestines, the brains fried in the skull itself. Is there anything more horrible than hell, boys? What can be more horrible than hell? When you go to your homes tonight, take icy cold showers and when you go to bed, lie on your backs with your hands folded in prayer above the blankets. And when Satan comes to tempt you with the sins of the flesh think of those two boys choking, gasping, screaming for mercy, doomed to hell for all eternity. God loves you, dear boys. *(pause)*

**FRANK.** *(sings)*
I AM A LITTLE CATHOLIC
I LOVE MY HOLY FAITH
AND I WILL BE TRUE TILL THE DAY I DIE
OR GO STRAIGHT DOWN TO HELL.

It wasn't easy becoming a little Catholic. Before our first communion we had to memorize the whole catechism, all the questions and all the answers and they were drilled into us by that schoolmaster, Mr. Glynn.

**MALACHY.** *(as Mr. Glynn)* McCourt, who made the world?

**FRANK.** God.

**MALACHY.** God, what?

**FRANK.** God, sir.

**MALACHY.** And who is God?

**FRANK.** God is the creator and sovereign lord of heaven and earth and of all things, sir.

**MALACHY.** And why did God make the world?

**FRANK.** God made the world so we'd all have something to stand on, sir.

**MALACHY.** There is something very strange about a boy who gives an answer like that, isn't there, boys?

**FRANK.** There is, sir. *(suddenly desperate because of the master's threatening look)* I know the seven deadly sins, sir.

**MALACHY.** Oh, you do, do you? And what is the first deadly sin?

**FRANK.** The pride, sir.

**MALACHY.** Ah, yes, the pride. If I catch a glint of pride in this class out comes the stick and there will be a smiting. What will there be, boys?

FRANK. A smiting, sir.

MALACHY. And what is the next deadly sin?

FRANK. The greed, sir.

MALACHY. Ah, the greed. There's a head that's bulging with the greed. *(pointing to Frank's head)* There's a head that will wind up in a hangman's knot at the end of a rope, the eyes bulging, the tongue dangling. And what's the next deadly sin?

FRANK. The lust, sir.

MALACHY. Ah, the lust. Well, we won't dawdle over that one, will we? You can always tell the one that's at the lust. At himself and interfering with himself. What is he, boys?

FRANK. At himself, sir.

MALACHY. And?

FRANK. Interfering with himself, sir.

MALACHY. And then comes the pimples. A half acre of pimples. And when I see a boy with the pimples, I will know. What will I know, boys?

FRANK. You'll know he has the pimples, sir.

MALACHY. No, you blithering idiots. I'll know he's been at himself. Then come the warts, squatting on the skin like dead lice. Between the warts and the pimples you can hardly tell whose face it is but we won't dwell on that, oh no, for that way madness lies, madness as Shakespeare says. Half the people above in the lunatic asylum are there because of the lust and you, McCourt, you're a prime candidate for the lust department of the lunatic asylum.

FRANK. *(fearing, again, the menacing master)* I know the best deadly sin.

MALACHY. The best deadly sin? And what might that be, pray?!

FRANK. It's the sloth: because the sloth is the laziness and the laziness is doing nothing and if you're doing nothing you can't be committing the other deadly sins, sir.

MALACHY. A theologian. Enough of the deadly sins. Now, McCourt, if you lead a good and virtuous life, what is the reward?

FRANK. The reward for leading a good and virtuous life is that you're admitted to heaven to stand before the throne of God, to gaze on his divine countenance for eternity in awe, wonder, and reverence, sir. *(pause)* Is that all?

MALACHY. Is what all?

FRANK. Is that all you get for leading a good and virtuous life? Standing there for eternity, looking at God's face. Wouldn't you get weary?

MALACHY. And what is it you want? Carnivals, circuses, naked dancing women. Before I'm done with you I'll teach you to love the gentle Jesus. Bend over.

FRANK. Help me now, Our Lady Queen of Knock.

MALACHY. *(striking with stick)* I'll give you knock.

*(blackout as stick is heard connecting)*

FRANK. We lived in the last house at the end of the lane. Next to our door was a shed. That was the lavatory. Not our lavatory. That was the lavatory for the whole lane. Sixteen families. They had to pass our door every day to empty their buckets of piss and shit. The worst bucket in the lane was Bawnie Sexton's. My father said the stink from Bawnie's bucket was cosmic. You could hang your hat on that stink. If that Winston Churchill had any sense he'd send Bawnie and her bucket over to that war going on in France. Make sure the wind was blowing in the right direction. "Bawnie, empty your bucket." she'd wipe out the whole German army. My father went to see the parish priest about that lavatory. He even went to see the mayor of Limerick himself, Dan Burke.

MALACHY. *(as the mayor, Dan Burke)* Ladies and Gentlemen and fellow-patriots, welcome to this extinguished assemblage. Let me reiterate what I am about to say. I see before me faces that are not here and I hope that those who are absent will take particular notice of my words today. I also miss some of the old faces I used to shake hands with. And I see before me faces I thought were dead and buried faces but thanks be to God they're alive and voting faces though mind you too many living people is not good business for the funeral undertakers of Limerick for they have little children and they need shoes too. That's what I'm here to talk to ye about today - the poor and the problem of shoes. The poor has always been with me. The poor has always been behind me. The poor has always voted for me, every man woman and child. Sure, there's nothing wrong with being poor as long as you vote for the right man. So it's my fond hope that you'll remain poor. And I promise when I'm reelected again I'll put shoes on all the poor, footless children of Limerick. It's not the poor that tells the lies about me. Oh. No. It's them snobs above on the hill. They have spread libel about me. They have spread scandal about me. They have even made allegations. I ask you: where are those libelers? Where are those scandalizers? Where are those alligators? They even said that if I were hanged for my intelligence I'd die completely innocent. That is a lie. Indeed half the lies they tell about me are not true and the other three quarters are exaggerated. I did my bit for Ireland and I see before me men standing who died for Ireland and they're walking around without jobs. I'm going to do something about that because I myself died for Ireland and if necessary I'll die again and again until I'm dead entirely.

FRANK. Dan. Where do you stand on the lavatories?

MALACHY. I'm behind the lavatories. There should be lavatories the length and breadth of Limerick. And not only should we build urinals for the men. We should construct arsenals for the women. I thank you.

FRANK. There was one day I was sure of getting a pair of shoes. My first communion day. The happiest day of life. Because after my first communion in the morning

I could go around to the neighbors and relations and make my collection money. Then in the afternoon I could go to the lyric cinema to see James Cagney. But my grandmother said:

MALACHY. *(as Grandmother)* No, your first Communion day is the happiest day of your life because on that day you receive on your tongue the body and blood of Jesus. That means you're a true Catholic. Now what can make you happier than that? Even if you won a million pounds in the Irish sweepstakes you couldn't be any happier.

FRANK. My happiest day. The night before I was so excited I couldn't sleep till dawn. I'd still be asleep if she hadn't come hammering at the door.

MALACHY. Get up. Get up. Get that child outta the bed. Happiest day of his life and him snoring above in the bed. Get him up. Take off that shirt!

FRANK. I jumped up. I ran to the kitchen. I took off the shirt and they threw me into a tin tub of icy cold water. My mother scrubbed me. My grandmother scrubbed me. I was raw. I was red. They dried me. They put on my First Communion suit, the lovely black velvet First Communion suit with the white frilly shirt, short pants, white stockings, black patent leather shoes, and around my arm they tied a white satin bow, and on my lapel they pinned the Sacred Heart of Jesus, with a crown of thorns dripping in blood, and the whole thing erupting in flames.

MALACHY. Come here, come here till I comb that hair. Look at that mop, it won't lie down. You didn't get that hair from my side of the family. That's that North of Ireland hair you got from your father. That's the kind of hair you see on Presbyterians. If your mother had married a decent Limerickman you wouldn't have that standing up, north of Ireland Presbyterian hair. *(She spits on his head.)*

FRANK. Grandma, will you please stop spitting on my head?

MALACHY. If you have anything to say, shut up. Come on.

FRANK. When we arrived at the church the last of the boys
was leaving the altar rail, where the priest stood there
holding the host and the chalice – glaring at me. Then
he placed on my tongue the wafer, the body and blood
of Jesus. At last. At last... It stuck. I had God glued to
the roof of my mouth. I could hear the schoolmaster's
voice...

MALACHY. (as Schoolmaster, offstage) Don't let the host touch
your teeth, for if you bite God in two you'll roast in
hell, for all eternity.

FRANK. I tried to get him down with my tongue. (makes a
clucking sound)

MALACHY. (as Priest) Stop that clucking and get back to
your seat.

FRANK. But God was good. He melted and came down.
Now at last, I was a true Catholic, and an official sinner.
When the mass was over there they were at the door,
my mother and my grandmother. My mother hugged
me and kissed me and cried all over my head and after
my grandmother's contribution that morning my head
was a swamp. Can I go now and make my collection?

MALACHY. (as Grandmother) You're not making no collection
till you've had a proper First Communion breakfast at
my house. Come on. (Grandmother in kitchen) I want you
to eat every scrap of that breakfast for there's many a
child in China would be glad for it.

FRANK. Can you name two of them? I ate the sausage, I ate
the egg, I ate the bread, and when I reached for more
sugar for my tea...

(Grandmother slaps his hand.)

MALACHY. Go aisy with that sugar. Is it a millionaire you
think I am, an American? Is it bedecked in glittering
jewelry you think I am, smothered in fancy furs?

FRANK. The food churned in my stomach. I ran to her
backyard and I threw it all up. Out she came.

**MALACHY.** Look what he did. Thrun up his First Communion breakfast. Thrun up the body and blood of Jesus. I have God in me backyard. Oh, what am I going to do? I know. I'll take him to the Jesuits, for the Jesuits hears the Pope's confession and when you know the Pope's sins you knows everything.

**FRANK.** She dragged me through the streets of Limerick and made me go to confession. In the name of the Father and of the Son and of the Holy Ghost. Bless me Father, for I have sinned. It's a day since my last confession. *(kneels at chair)*

**MALACHY.** *(as Priest)* And what sins did you commit in one day, my son?

**FRANK.** I overslept. My grandmother said I had standing up North of Ireland Presbyterian hair. I threw up my First Communion breakfast. Now she says she has God in her backyard and what should she do?

**MALACHY.** *(as Priest, laughing)* Ah, tell your grandmother to wash God away with a little water, and for your penance say a prayer for me.

*(as Grandmother)* Were you telling jokes to that priest in the confession box? If 'tis a thing I ever hear you were telling jokes to Jesuits I'll tear the bloody kidneys outa you. Now what did he say about God in me backyard?

**FRANK.** *(stands)* He said wash him away with a little water, Grandma.

**MALACHY.** Holy water or ordinary water?

**FRANK.** He didn't say, Grandma.

**MALACHY.** Well, go back and axe him.

**FRANK.** But Grandma!

*(**MALACHY**, as Grandmother, points sternly to confession box)*

**FRANK.** *(kneels, back in the confession box)* Bless me, Father, for I have sinned. It's a minute since my last confession.

**MALACHY.** *(as Priest)* Are you the child who was just here?

FRANK. I am, Father.

MALACHY. *(as priest)* Well, what is it now?

FRANK. My grandma says holy water or ordinary water.

MALACHY. She can pass her own water for all I care, just tell her stop bothering me.

FRANK. He said you can pass your own water for all he cares and he said don't be botherin' him again.

MALACHY. *(as Grandmother)* Don't be botherin' him again. That bloody, ignorant bogtrotter. Well, I won't rest, so I won't. I won't rest till the Bishop of Limerick comes here in his vestments and accoutrements and consecrates my backyard and causes to be erected here a holy shrine in memory of the day that my grandson, my own flesh and blood, threw up the body and blood of Jesus, the only begotten son of our Lady, queen of knock.

*(blackout)*

FRANK. The outside world rarely came to the lane though there was one man who came every week, the insurance man, Mr. Higgins. My grandmother said, "Insurance is a gorgeous thing to have for with the insurance you're sure of a grave in consecrated ground. That means you have the dignity and you can hold your head up."

MALACHY. Hold your head up, indeed.

FRANK. Said my father.

MALACHY. *(as father)* When you're six feet under. The day I die they can put me face down in the coffin and the insurance man can kiss my dead Irish arse.

FRANK. My mother wanted the insurance but she didn't always have the money for it so when Mr. Higgins came she'd have to hide.

MALACHY. *(as Insurance Man, sings)*
FOR THERE'S NO ONE WITH ENDURANCE
LIKE THE MAN WHO SELLS INSURANCE!
HE'S EVERYBODY'S BEST FRIEND.
Insurance, please. Pay up, Mrs. McCourt. I know you're

in there, lurking and skulking. But lurk and skulk as ye may. The insurance must be paid. Pay up,

**FRANK.** Me mother says she's out.

**MALACHY.** Out is she? Well, ask your mother that's out when she'll be in?

**FRANK.** It may be for years and it may be forever.

**MALACHY.** And it may be too late. Do ye want to be taken away in an ass and cart when ye die? Or is it dumped in the bogs like decomposin' dogs ye want to be? Or, God save us and guard us, is it buried in unconsecrated ground with Protestants, Jews, and vegetarians ye want to be?

**FRANK.** (as Mother) No. No. Here's your money. God above, the things I have to give up for this bloody insurance. You are worse than the forty days of Lent!

**MALACHY.** You won't be sorry, Mrs. McCourt, you won't be sorry. The day you die you'll get down on your two knees and you'll thank God for a holy, decent and Catholic burial...

For there's no one with endurance like the man who sells insurance. He's everybody's best friend.

**BOTH.** (as women from the lane)
WE ARE TWO LOVELY LASSIES FROM LIMERICK LIMERICK, LIMERICK.
WE ARE TWO LOVELY LASSIES FROM LIMERICK.
AND I AM THE BEST OF THEM ALL.

**MALACHY.** I didn't see you at the novena to Our Lady of Perpetual Succor last night.

**FRANK.** How could you? I wasn't there. I was at a wake.

**MALACHY.** A wake? Whose wake was that and why wasn't I axed?

**FRANK.** A lovely wake it was for little Jack McQuiggan that died till that Michael McGuire came in langers drunk, started singing without an invitation, dancing like a whirling dervish without a partner. The next thing - he had a heart attack and he dropped down dead. He ruined the whole wake.

MALACHY. Oh, another wake. Do you know who else died?

FRANK. No. Who?

MALACHY. The boy of the O'Grady's above in Garryowen.

FRANK. Oh? An' what did he die of?

MALACHY. Oh, 'twas nothing serious.

FRANK. Thank God for that.

MALACHY. Lovely boy he was, an Irish mother's dream. Always on his bended knees. Never went out with girls. Never touched himself in an impure manner. An' didn't he die in a state of grace in his mother's arms.

FRANK. She must be delirious with the joy over the way he went with the purity an' all, they'll have a wake, of course.

MALACHY. Indeed they will. Sure isn't there loads of insurance in that family. Lashings of food an' barrels of beer an' cakes an' sausages an' big bowls of mustard to clear the head, pipes of tobacco, sauces of snuff, and bottles of the hard stuff.

FRANK. An' Gurky will be there telling his stories.

MALACHY. He will, indeed.

FRANK. I'll see you at the wake then, missus.

MALACHY. Get there early for that Gurky has a thirst on him like a camel.

BOTH. *(singing)*

AN' I AM THE BEST OF THEM ALL

MALACHY. *(as Gurky)* How are ye? Lovely wake, eh? Your man in the bed there. Grand man he was. Healthy as a trout. Used to be a sailor like meself. Oh, I was indeed. Sure, wasn't I on them sailing ships in me youth before ye were born. Begod I was, swoopin' around the Cape of Good Horn. An' didn't the captain say to me, 'Gurky, climb up to the top of that mast an' light the storm lantern... Aye, Aye, sir, sez I, for if I didn't he'd hang me from the same mast for mutiny, him being a Born Again Christian and an Englishman. So, I took my box of matches an' up the riggin' with me.

Up an' up I climbed an' when I reached the top didn't
I waste nearly the whole box of matches tryin' to light
that bloody lantern. By this time a storm was roarin'
out of the south pole, drivin' clouds across the moon
an' blackenin' the sky so there wasn't a star to be seen
for love nor sausages. The wind howled like a banshee
an' I said to meself, 'Gurky, get down off this.' A third
of the way down the mast didn't a great blast of wind
sweep in an' whirl all the sails away into the blackness
of the night like poor souls sucked into eternity, God
save the mark. The mast was buckin' back an' forth.
The waves was comin' this way, the wind was comin'
this way an' I'm tryin' to stay where I am. Inchin' me
way down the mast, foot by foot, I got down to the
bottom of the mast an' there was the friggin' ship...
Gone! ...I'd like to know what ye are laughin' at. 'Tis a
serious matter to lose a ship when you're on it.

*(sings)*
WE HAD SAILED SEVEN YEARS WHEN THE MEASLES BROKE
    OUT
AND THE SHIP LOST ITS WAY IN A FOG
THEN THE WHALE OF A CREW WAS
REDUCED DOWN TO TWO
MESELF AND THE CAPTAIN' S OLD DOG.
THEN THE SHIP HIT A ROCK
OH, LORD, WHAT A SHOCK
THE BOAT IT TURNED RIGHT OVER
WHIRLED NINE TIMES AROUND
AND THE POOR OLD DOG WAS DROWNED
I'M THE LAST OF THE IRISH ROVERS.

FRANK. People were always dying in the lane. Our sister,
Margaret, died at six months. Our brother, Eugene,
died of diphtheria when he was four. A few months
later his twin, Oliver, died.

MALACHY. It was a bright and sunny day when Oliver died.
You could hardly see his body in the bed with the
whiteness of everything: the whiteness of the sheets,
the whiteness of the pillowcase, the whiteness of the

habit he wore. A long smelly man came into the room and he went over to where Oliver was laid out on the bed. He took a piece of string out of his pocket and measured him from head to foot and he left. "Dad, what was that smelly man doing to Oliver?" "Shhhh... Oliver is gone off to heaven to play with the baby Jesus..." "Will I have to go to heaven and play with the baby Jesus, Dad?" "No, you won't. Just say a prayer that Oliver is happy in heaven."

I knelt down beside Oliver's body but I couldn't think of a prayer... I shook him... Wake up, Oliver, wake up an' we'll play horsey... He took no notice of me... Tickle, tickle, tickle, Oliver... The next thing I got a thump on the side of the head... There was my grandmother standing over me screaming, "I'll give you tickle, tickle, you little blaguard. I'll give you who began it for disturbing the dead." I ran into the kitchen thinking if heaven was such a grand place why didn't my grandmother scoot off there and not be bothering me. When I heard her leaving I came back out. After a while the smelly man returned. He was carrying a white box that had brass handles on it. He put it on the floor and took the cover off. That started my mother off. "Oh, sweet Jesus, don't take him from me. Mother of God, help me." My father lifted Oliver off the bed and put him in the box.

My father, with the tears streaming down his face, had to push her away so the smelly man could put the cover on, and he clamped it down with brass screws that had heads in the shape of a cross. He and my father carried the box outside, followed by Frank and myself dressed in our Sunday suits. There outside was a big, black carriage drawn by a lovely white horse. Inside, across the two seats, was the white box. We got in, set off down the town feeling very proud riding in that carriage looking out the window, hoping all our pals would see us, but they're never around when you want them. When the carriage stopped we were in an old overgrown graveyard. My father and the smelly man took the white box over to where two men were standing, leaning on shovels beside a very deep hole in the ground with a big pile of earth beside it that smelled very nice. They lowered the box into the hole, threw some freshly cut grass on it and some sods that went "thunk" as they hit the coffin. The two men filled in the rest of the hole. There were no prayers for small children then. Anyway, we couldn't afford a priest. We just walked back to the carriage, got in, and the ride home was very short because the horse trotted all the way. When we turned the corner into our lane there was a game of soccer going on with all our pals. My father told Frank and myself go off and play till supper time and we did and the boys let us score a lot of goals because our brother had just died.

**FRANK.** After Oliver died my father told us no more stories. He sang now only when he was drunk.

**BOTH.** *(sing)*

SOME SAY THE DEVIL'S DEAD, DEVIL'S DEAD, DEVIL'S DEAD.
SOME SAY THE DEVIL'S DEAD AND BURIED IN KILLARNEY.
MORE SAY HE ROSE AGAIN, MORE SAY HE ROSE AGAIN,
MORE SAY HE ROSE AGAIN AND JOINED THE BRITISH ARMY.

**FRANK.** My mother did nothing all day but sit gazing into the fire. Nobody paid us a scrap of attention.

**MALACHY.** We could do anything we liked. We could sing our own songs. Play our own games... Let's play wake for Oliver.

**FRANK.** How do you play wake, Malachy?

**MALACHY.** The big people sing and drink and dance all night.

**BOTH.** *(singing and dancing)*

THERE'S A BIG SHIP SAILING ON THE ILLY ALLY O
ILLY ALLY O, ILLY ALLY O
THERE'S A BIG SHIP SAILING ON THE ILLY ALLY O
HEY, HO, ILLY ALLY O.

*(Now they sing. Alternating verses)*

**FRANK.**

THERE WAS AN OLD WOMAN WHO LIVED IN THE WOODS
WEELA WEELA WALLIA
THERE WAS AN OLD WOMAN WHO LIVED IN THE WOODS
DOWN BY THE RIVER SALLIA.

**MALACHY.**

SHE HAD A BABY SIX MONTHS OLD
WEELA WEELA WALLIA
SHE HAD A BABY SIX MONTHS OLD
DOWN BY THE RIVER SALLIA.

**FRANK.**

SHE HAD A PENKNIFE LONG AND SHARP
WEELA WEELA WALLIA
SHE HAD A PENKNIFE LONG AND SHARP
DOWN BY THE RIVER SALLIA.

**MALACHY.**

SHE STUCK THE KNIFE IN THE BABY'S HEAD
WEELA WEELA WALLIA
SHE STUCK THE KNIFE IN THE BABY'S HEAD
DOWN BY THE RIVER SALLIA.

**FRANK.**

THERE CAME THREE MEN A KNOCKIN' AT THE DOOR
WEELA WEELA WALLIA
TWO POLICEMEN AND A MAN
DOWN BY THE RIVER SALLIA.

**MALACHY.**

ARE YOU THE WOMAN WHAT KILLED THE CHILD?
WEELA WEELA WALLIA
ARE YOU THE WOMAN WHAT KILLED THE CHILD?
DOWN BY THE RIVER SALLIA.

**FRANK.**

I AM THE WOMAN WHAT KILLED THE CHILD
WEELA WEELA WALLIA
I AM THE WOMAN WHAT KILLED THE CHILD
DOWN BY THE RIVER SALLIA.

THEY TOOK A ROPE AND THEY HUNG HER UP
WEELA WEELA WALLIA
THEY TOOK A ROPE AND THEY HUNG HER UP
DOWN BY THE RIVER SALLIA.

**MALACHY.**

> NOW THAT WAS THE END OF THE WOMAN IN THE WOODS
> WEELA WEELA WALLIA
> THAT WAS THE END OF THE BABY, TOO
> DOWN BY THE RIVER SALLIA.

**BOTH.**

> THE MORAL OF THIS STORY IS
> WEELA WEELA WALLIA
> DON'T STICK KNIVES IN BABIES' HEADS
> DOWN BY THE RIVER SALLIA.

**MALACHY.** Sing us something sad, Frank.

**FRANK.** *(Sings)*

> HAVE YOU HEARD OF PHIL THE FLUTHER
> OF THE TOWN OF BALLYMUCK
> THE TIMES WERE GOING HARD FOR HIM
> IN FACT THE MAN WAS BRUK
> AND SO HE JUST SENT OUT A NOTICE
> TO HIS NEIGHBORS ONE AND ALL
> AS HOW HE'D LIKE THEIR COMPANY
> THAT EVENING AT A BALL.
> AND WHEN WRIT'ING OUT
> HE WAS CAREFUL TO SUGGEST TO THEM
> THAT IF THEY FOUND A HAT OF HIS
> CONVENIENT TO THE DOOR,
> THE MORE THEY PUT IN
> WHENEVER HE REQUESTED IT
> THE BETTER WOULD THE MUSIC BE
> FOR BATTERING ON THE FLOOR
> WITH A TOOT ON THE FLUTE AND A TWIDDLE ON THE
>     FIDDLE O
> HOPPING WITH THE FIDDLE LIKE A HERRING ON THE
>     GRIDDLE O
> UP DOWN HANDS AROUND AND HOPPING TO THE WALL
> OH, HADN'T WE THE GAIETY AT PHIL THE FLUTHER' S BALL.
>
> THERE WAS MISTER DENIS DOUGHERTY
> WHO KEPT THE RUNNING DOG.
> LITTLE CROOKED PADDY FROM THE TIRALOGHET BOG
> THERE WERE BOYS FROM EVERY BARONY

GIRLS FROM EVERY ART AND THE BEAUTIFUL MISS BRADYS
IN THEIR PRIVATE ASS AND CART.
AND ALONG WITH THEM
CAME THE BOUNCING MRS. CAFFERTY
LITTLE MICKEY MULLIGAN
WAS ALSO TO THE FORE.
ROSE, SUZANNE AND MARGARET O'RAFFERTY
THE FLOWER OF ADRAMGULLION
AND THE PRIDE OF PETRAVORE.
WITH A TOOT ON THE FLUTE AND A TWIDDLE ON THE
    FIDDLE O
HOPPING WITH THE FIDDLE LIKE A HERRING ON THE
    GRIDDLE O
UP DOWN HANDS AROUND, CROSSING TO THE WALL
OH, HADN'T WE THE GAIETY AT PHIL THE FLUTHER'S BALL.

FIRST LITTLE MICKEY MULLIGAN GOT UP TO SHOW THEM
    HOW
THEN THE WIDOW CAFFERTY STARTS UP AND MAKES HER
    BOW.
I CAN DANCE YOU OFF YOUR LEGS, SEZ SHE,
AS SURE AS YOU WERE BORN
IF YOU'LL ONLY MAKE THE PIPER PLAY
THE HARE WAS IN THE CORN.
SO PHIL PLAYED UP TO THE BEST OF HIS ABILITY
THE LADY AND THE GENTLEMAN
BEGAN TO DO THEIR SHARE.
FAITH THEN, MICK, IT'S YOU THAT HAS AGILITY.
BEGORRAH, MRS. CAFFERTY, YOU'RE LEPPIN' LIKE A HARE.
WITH A TOOTLE ON THE FLUTEL
AND A TWIDDLE ON THE FIDDLE O
HOPPIN' WITH THE FIDDLE
LIKE A HERRING ON THE GRIDDLE O
UP DOWN HANDS AROUND
CROSSING TO THE WALL.
OH HAD'T WE THE GAIETY
AT PHIL THE FLUTHER'S BALL.

And that is the official Irish sobriety test.

**MALACHY.** *(sings)*
    IN KILKENNY IT IS REPORTED
    THEY HAVE MARBLE STONE THERE
    AS BLACK AS INK.
    WITH GOLD AND SILVER
    I DID SUPPORT HER.
    AND I'LL SING NO MORE NOW
    TILL I GET A DRINK.
    FOR I'M DRUNK TODAY
    AND I'M SELDOM SOBER
    A HANDSOME ROVER FROM
    TOWN TO TOWN.
    AH, BUT I AM SICK NOW
    MY DAYS ARE NUMBERED
    COME ALL YE YOUNG GIRLS
    AND LAY ME DOWN.

**FRANK.** *(in Irish\*)*
    NI RAIMID ABAILE GO MAIDIN

*(MALACHY joins in.)*
    NI RAIMID ABAILE GO MAIDIN
    NI RAIMID ABAILE GO MAIDIN
    NI RAIMID ABAILE GO DEO.

**FRANK.** ...and they all talk the same when someone dies.

*(They stand, don shawls and become women.)*

**MALACHY.** Very sorry for your troubles, missus.

**FRANK.** I know you are, missus.

**MALACHY.** Your poor husband. Dead as a mackerel in the bed. Grand man he was.

**FRANK.** Indeed an' he was.

**MALACHY.** Lovely head o' hair he had, black and curly an' not a smidgen of gray in it.

**FRANK.** The lovliest head of hair in the lane. Gone forever from my snowy white pillow.

---

\* *(Translation)*
    Oh, we won't go home until morning
    We won't go home until morning
    We won't go home until morning
    We won't go home at all.

MALACHY. Grand figure of a man he was too, the shoulders on him.

FRANK. Oh, the shoulders, indeed the shoulders and head gone forever from my pillow.

MALACHY. Shoulders that wide he had to come in the door of sideways.

FRANK. Bruises he had on his shoulders from trying to come in the door like an ordinary man.

MALACHY. A grand man he was.

FRANK. My husband that's dead there in the bed could sing the *Rose of Tralee* with the best of them. Wasn't John McCormack eaten up with the envy. Eaten up he was. My husband was a good Catholic too. For ever fingering his beads. The knees of his trousers worn out with the praying.

MALACHY. A good Catholic indeed and I for one never believed what they said about him and the sheep.

FRANK. If I ever doubted that he has a bed in heaven it would shake my faith and drive me to eating sausages on Friday.

malachy. Above all, missus, above all the lovliest thing you can say about any Irish man including your poor dead mackerel in the bed is he was always good to his mother.

BOTH. *(sing)*
A MOTHER'S LOVE IS A BLESSING
NO MATTER WHERE YOU ROAM
KEEP HER WHILE YOU HAVE HER
YOU WILL MISS HER WHEN SHE'S GONE
LOVE HER AS IN CHILDHOOD
THOUGH FEEBLE OLD AND GRAY
FOR YOU'LL NEVER MISS A MOTHER'S LOVE
'TILL SHE'S BURIED BENEATH THE CLAY.

MALACHY. Sometimes we didn't go home and sometimes we didn't go to school.

FRANK. When I'm big I'll get a job and every Saturday I am going to the Lyric Cinema to see Boy and Jane and Tarzan.

MALACHY. *(as Priest)* You're not supposed to see Tarzan.

FRANK. Oh, Father Gorey again.

MALACHY. That apostle of paganism, free love, and irre-sponsibility. Do you see Tarzan putting on a collar and tie of a Monday and looking for a job for himself?

FRANK. No.

MALACHY. Do you see Tarzan going to mass of a Sunday?

FRANK. No.

MALACHY. Do you see Tarzan getting married in the One, Holy, Roman Catholic and Apostolic church?

FRANK. Of course not.

MALACHY. That Tarzan is in a constant state of sin, a sin of the flesh. What if him and Jane were there in the jungle and she fell off one of them swinging vines…

FRANK. She wouldn't have far to fall from his old vine.

MALACHY. You dirty thing. Do you know what it is that's ruining the children of Limerick? It's sitting in the cinemas hour after hour watching eejits flying through the air with no visible means of support, singing cowboys and naked dancing girls. I will not preside over the californication of the children of Limerick.

FRANK. I'm going to the Lyric Cinema to see all the Rogerses: buck Rogers flying, Roy Rogers riding, Ginger Rogers dancing.

MALACHY. Ginger Rogers! Ginger Rogers is an occasion of sin. Leppin' around there with scarcely as much clothes as would stuff a crutch. Catholic boys should avoid the dancing because dancing is also dangerous to your health because dancing causes dust to rise from the floor. That dust settles in the lungs and causes consumption, galloping consumption. Therefore, not only is Ginger Rogers an occasion of sin, she's the direct cause of galloping consumption in all of Ireland.

FRANK. I'm still going to the Lyric Cinema even though the ticket man is always yelling at us. "Boys on one side, girls on the other."

MALACHY. But she's me financee.

FRANK. *(as Ticket Man)* I wouldn't care if she was your grandmother. This picture house is not going to be no randyboo. There is to be no calling back and forth. There is to be no swapping of spits. There is to be no cheerin' for divorced film stars. There is to be no cheerin' for them naked red Indians. They're not Catholics.

MALACHY. Hey, Cochise, scalp the soldiers.

FRANK. I said: no cheerin' for them naked red Indians. They're killing the United States Calvary up there an' half o' them are Irish.

MALACHY. Sitting Bull! In the name of Jesus, will you get up off your arse an' use your tommy-hawk.

FRANK. I said, no cheerin' for them naked red Indians. You can cheer for Errol Flynn, good Irishman.

MALACHY. Errol Flynn is divorced.

FRANK. Is he? Is he? Well, cheer for the feckin Indians.

MALACHY. *(as Convict in prison)* Don't come in, Warden. Hey, Warden, we don't wanna hurt you, Warden.

FRANK. James Cagney? I'm sending in the priest.

MALACHY. Pat O'Brien? Don't come in here. The food stinks.

FRANK. I don't care. I'm coming in anyway.

MALACHY. Aw, Fadder, Fadder, Fadder.

FRANK. Aw, Rocky, Rocky, Rocky.

MALACHY. I'm gonna fry in the electric chair tonight, Fadder.

FRANK. Oh, you're gonna fry tonight, Rocky. That reminds me; what would you like for your last meal?

MALACHY. I'd like some pea soup like my mother used to make. I'd like a baked potato, Fadder and I'd like a steak that thick.

FRANK. I'm sorry, Rocky. It's Friday. Go in peace with the potato, Rocky. Wait a minute. Did you say pea soup, a baked potato, and a steak that thick?

MALACHY. Yeah.

FRANK. I'd die for that.

MALACHY. So would I.

FRANK. Move over.

*(sits next to* MALACHY *while they simulate execution)*

If I didn't have the money to go to the Lyric Cinema on a Saturday I could go instead to the new Children's Library... excuse me, miss. Could I please join the library?

MALACHY. *(as Librarian)* What is your name?

FRANK. Frank McCourt, miss.

MALACHY. And where do you live?

FRANK. Schoolhouse lane, miss.

MALACHY. *(to off)* Oh, Dymphna. There's one of them here. The lower classes want to read books, mind you. Next thing they'll rise up in revolution, come in here with swords in their hands, to cut our heads off and throw them on that table to stare us in the face.

FRANK. Oh, St. Dymphna is the patron saint of lunatics.

MALACHY. Then she'd be the proper patron saint for *your* family. Let me see those paws. Filthy. Disgusting. Go wash those filthy paws.

FRANK. I washed my hands in the gutter rainwater. *(returns and shows hands to librarian)*

MALACHY. This is a book. It is for reading, mind you. Its pages are not for lighting your cigarettes or wiping your laners arse.

FRANK. It was the first book of my life, a lovely book, lavishly illustrated, "Stories Of The Great Operas." I sat in the kitchen reading n' and I was in heaven, even if my Grandmother was here. And I read all about La Bohemee, Calvary Rustiana, Die Fieldmouse, and my favorite, Ayda. *(rhymes with "payda")* they buried her and her lover alive in a tomb. *(sings)* Celeste AYda... Stop the singing, Aida. You'll use up all the air in the tomb and you'll be dead.

MALACHY. *(as Grandmother)* What in God's name are you whingin' about? Is your bladder near your eye?

FRANK. It's Ayda.

MALACHY. Ida? Ida who? Is it Ida lynch above in Garryowen?

FRANK. She's an Egyptian.

MALACHY. An Egyptian. What in God's name are you bawling over Egyptians for? Isn't there enough to bawl about in your own unfortunate family? Cry for your father that can't get a job and has to go to work in England.

MALACHY. Goodbye, Dad.

FRANK. Goodbye, Dad.

MALACHY. Send money, Dad.

FRANK. Don't forget the money, Dad.

MALACHY. Goodbye, Mr. Meehan.

FRANK. Goodbye, Mr. Sheehan.

MALACHY. Goodbye, Mr. Horrigan.

FRANK. Goodbye, Mr. Henaghan.

*(MALACHY and FRANK as women in the lane:)*

MALACHY. Isn't it very strange there are some an' their husbands are gone off to England to join the British army after what the English did to the Irish for eight long centuries.

FRANK. There are some that don't mind if their husbands sit on their arses in the kitchen, readin' the paper an' waitin' for the streets to be well aired before they take a little stroll down the town lookin' for work an' hopin' to God they won't find it.

MALACHY. There's nobody in my family looks like a Black and Tan. But there are some that are livin' off the British army pension because she claims her husband was wounded in the war. Wounded he was an' him runnin' from the enemy and the backs of his legs being penetrated by his own hard balls of shit.

**FRANK.** There's one that I won't even mention. She's known all over as the town bicycle for there isn't a man standin' in Limerick that didn't have a good ride on her.

**MALACHY.** There's some that can talk that have a daughter wanderin' around, painted and powdered and rouged, a flaghoppin' streetwalkin' wanton strap of a streetwalker, she spends so much time down the docks on her back on the flat of her back, attractin' and wreckin' foreign sailors she's known all over as Limerick's harbor light.

**FRANK.** Daughters is it? Daughters? There's some that have twin daughters that Irish Catholic names are not good enough for them. Oh, no. They have to christen the little girls after what they think is two Italian saints, syphilis and gonorrhea.

**MALACHY.** God blast your cheek. May your husband be standin' sentry duty at Buckingham palace an' may the king of England's horse fart in his face.

**FRANK.** And you. May you swallow your tongue. May it travel the length of your insides and may you spend the rest of your days talkin' through the hole of your arse.

**BOTH.** *(sing)*
AND I AM THE BEST OF THEM ALL.

**MALACHY.** Goodbye, Frank.

**FRANK.** Goodbye, Malachy.

**MALACHY.** Send American money, Frank.

**FRANK.** I will, Malachy.

**MALACHY.** Oh, watch out for those American girls.

**FRANK.** Why?

**MALACHY.** I hear there's no chastity in New York.

**FRANK.** Thank God for that.

**MALACHY.** And get yourself a Presbyterian.

**FRANK.** Why?

**MALACHY.** She'll go with your hair.

*(sings)*

GOODBYE TO ALL THE BOYS AT HOME,
HE'S SAILING FAR ACROSS THE FOAM
TO TRY TO SEEK HIS FORTUNE
IN FAR AMERIKAY.

THERE"S GOLD AND MONEY PLENTY
FOR THE POOR AND FOR THE GENTRY
THE NEXT TIME THAT YOU SEE HIM
HE'LL BE IN AMERIKAY

# ACT II

MALACHY. *(as woman, singing)*
OH, GOODBYE, JOHNNY DEAR, WHEN YOU'RE FAR AWAY,
DON'T FORGET YOUR DEAR OLD MOTHER FAR ACROSS THE
SEA.
WRITE A LETTER NOW AND THEN, SEND HER ALL YOU CAN,
AND DON'T FORGET WHERE'ER YOU ROAM THAT YOU'RE
AN IRISHMAN.

FRANK. How could I forget? They wouldn't let me. When I came here the old timer said

MALACHY. It ain't goin' to be easy, kid. This isn't the old country, you know. This is America. You can't be sittin' on your ass, day in, day out, dreamin'. Who do you think built this country?

FRANK. The Chinese might have driven a few spikes in the Central Pacific railroad. Blacks might have picked a little cotton and hoisted a few bales. German, Poles and Italians might have sweated a bit here and there. But... who built the skyscrapers? Who dug the canals? Who built the Catholic church? Who got the most medals of honor? Who designed the White House? America, I discovered, was essentially an Irish venture. So...with Eisenhower in the White House enjoying the fruits of Irish architectural genius, all the medals of honor secured by Audie Murphy and the fighting sixty-ninth, America all built, there was nothing left for me to do... But the old timer said:

MALACHY. The thing for him to do now is to get the high school diploma for it's easy to see from the dopey look on his kisser he don't have one. That way he can join the cops.

FRANK. The cops!

37

MALACHY. The cops. You can have the pension, the secu-
rity, the uniform, the dignity, the shoes but, above all...
You're with your own.

FRANK. My own! Had I traveled three thousand miles
across the Atlantic to be with my own? Was I to stand
on some bleak street corner dreaming of a pension,
swinging a nightstick to eternity? But... the old timer
said,

MALACHY. Stick with your own. Stick with your own.

FRANK. And so, for the want of something better to do, I
wrote my brother Malachy and asked him to join me in
New York. But I wasn't here to greet him. The United
States Army had already greeted me and invited me
to help defend the American way of life. I defended
democracy - in the beer halls of Bavaria.

*(sings and marches)*

YOU HAD A GOOD HOME AND YOU LEFT, YOU'RE RIGHT.
YOU HAD A GOOD HOME AND YOU LEFT, YOU'RE RIGHT.
YOU HAD A GOOD HOME AND YOU LEFT, YOU'RE RIGHT.
JUDY WAS THERE WHEN YOU LEFT, YOU'RE RIGHT.

Far from my own - and glad of it, I roistered my days
away till one night at a party in Munich I met an
American army librarian.

*(to* MALACHY, *as Librarian)* God, you're a lovely looking
girl with that red hair tumbling down your back like
the sun kissing the river Shannon at twilight...

MALACHY. Oh, you're Irish!

FRANK. I admitted it.

MALACHY. And what do you think of Joyce?

FRANK. Joyce? I haven't met her yet. Is she here?

MALACHY. I mean James Joyce. Your most eminent Irish
author.

FRANK. I never heard of him.

MALACHY. You're Irish and you've never heard of James
Joyce! Why we studied him for a whole year at Vassar.

FRANK. She was a lovely looking librarian and I thought if I could become familiar with the works of this James Joyce I might become intimate with the librarian... I went to the library. This looks like a lively James Joyce book, "Finnegan's Wake." I always liked wakes. *(reads)* "Riverrun, past Adam and Eve's, from swerve of shore to bend of bay brings us by a commodious vicus of recirculation back to Howth castle and environs." This is gibberish. Was this Joyce drunk when he wrote this book?

MALACHY. *(as Librarian)* Oh, no. Joyce knew exactly what he was doing. You must persevere. Come to my apartment tonight and I'll explain Joyce to you.

FRANK. I did. She did. She told me all about James Joyce and William Butler Yeats and Oscar Wilde and she gave me lessons in love and affection. Pamela.

MALACHY. Yes.

FRANK. Why are you so interested in the Irish writers?

MALACHY. The Irish writers are the most important since the Elizabethans.

FRANK. Are the Elizabethans important, Pamela?

MALACHY. Very important. And I'll tell you more after I tinkle.

FRANK. That settled it. I was learning the importance of being important... That librarian was on to something and what was I but an illiterate poltroon from Limerick reading Joyce only to insinuate myself into her bed. And there in the hills of Bavaria I at last became an Irishman. I don't know what I was before then but the librarian assured me I had suffered a massive identity crisis. My God, I said, surely it wasn't that bad.

MALACHY. "Worse. You didn't know yourself. You didn't know your heritage. Now when you go back to New York you'll be a real person. Now you have roots. Oh, I wish I had roots like yours."

FRANK. I offered to share the main root with her... Trailing my roots I returned to New York, a newly minted mick, ready now to stick with my own. If you're Irish in New York and you want to stick with your own you can do it in the churches, the dance halls, the bars. Churches? I was too far gone in the seven deadly sins. So I danced. There are thirty two counties in Ireland. They all have dances in New York. I went to all of them. There were the girls, ranged along the wall–platoons of Celtic chastity, with Toni perms you couldn't shift with a jack-hammer.

FRANK. Excuse me, miss. Would you like to dance?

MALACHY. No, tanks. I'm taken.

FRANK. Excuse me, miss. Would you like to dance?

MALACHY. Axe me sister. I'm sweatin'.

FRANK. Excuse me, miss. Would you like to dance?

MALACHY. I will - but you keep your hands in a pure, chaste, and proper place above the waist.

*(He mimes dancing with partner.)*

FRANK. Do you come here often?

MALACHY. I do - when there's a dance.

FRANK. Do you like dancing?

MALACHY. I do - with them that knows how.

FRANK. *(getting desperate)* Would you... Would you like to go home with me tonight?

MALACHY. I will not. I was at confession today and I'm receiving in the morning.

FRANK. Wouldn't you like to receive tonight?

What was the use? They were all waiting there for someone significant, someone with a civil service job and a pension. And what if they asked me what I did for a living? Was I to tell them about my new job at the Biltmore hotel where I built speaker's platforms for dinners and banquets? I gave it up. I gave up the danc-ing and I took up the drinking. I drank along Third Avenue from fourteenth street to eighty-sixth street

and after my long nights on Third Avenue when I got
into that hotel in the morning I was so weary I took
short cuts with the supports under the speaker's platform. Till one day there was a lunch for very important
insurance executives and when the chairman of the
board got up to make his speech the platform col-
lapsed and on his way to the hospital he had a heart
attack and he died.

*(Sings)*

FOR THERE'S NO ONE WITH ENDURANCE
LIKE THE MAN WHO SELLS INSURANCE
HE'S EVERYBODY'S BEST FRIEND.
My boss, Mr. Carey, sent for me.

**MALACHY.** *(as Mr. Carey)* McCourt, if you weren't one of my
own I'd kick your ass all the back to Limerick. That's
it, kid. We're taking you away from anything to do with
human beings. We're putting you in charge of the
birds.

**FRANK.** The birds! Sixty canaries in their cages. It was my
job to climb up, feed them, water them, clean their
cages, look for signs of canary melancholy. I was good
at that job but then my social career began to inter-
fere with my canary career and after my long nights on
Third Avenue, when I got into that hotel in the morning, the last thing I wanted to see or hear was sixty
chattering, chirping canaries. Instead of taking care
of them I took naps. When I came out of my naps I
began to find some of the canaries lying at the bottom
of their cages - dead. If Mr. Carey found out I'd be out
of a job. I climbed my ladder. I took the dead canaries and I glued them to their perches. They weren't
singing much but they could be seen and my job was
secure for a while. Till my first St. Patrick's Day in New
York I went to a dance and I fell in with a nymphoma-
niac from Killarney. I thought I was taking her home.
She took me home. We frolicked in her place from the
seventeenth of March, which is the feast of St. Patrick,
till the nineteenth of march, the feast of St. Joseph.
Philomena, I have to go.

MALACHY. Go? I'm barely started.

FRANK. But, Philomena, I have a job.

MALACHY. Job! You didn't do much of a job here. I'd get more lovin' from a dead Republican.

FRANK. How can you say that after I've given of myself unstintingly from the feast of St. Patrick to the feast of St. Joseph? Besides, I have to take care of the canaries.

MALACHY. That's about the size of it. *(looking at his crotch)* You care more for them canaries than you do for me.

FRANK. If that was the case, Philomena, you'd be dead.

MALACHY. Holy mother of Jesus, a mass murderer.

FRANK. Back at the hotel there was a note on my time clock, report at once to Mr. Carey.

MALACHY. *(as Mr. Carey)* Kid, what did you do to the birds?

FRANK. What birds, Mr. Carey?

MALACHY. I'm not talking about the goddam swallows of Capistrano. I'm talking about thirty nine canaries dead in their cages.

FRANK. Oh, they must have died while I was out, Mr. Carey.

MALACHY. Oh, yeah. An' what did they do - get up an' glue themselves to their perches before they died? That's it, kid. First, the chairman of the board, now thirty-nine canaries. You know something, kid. You have a talent. You're a real killer. You ought a go an' get a job as an exterminator.

FRANK. Enough. Enough. No more Irish bars. No more Irish dances. No more Irish nymphomaniacs. Miss? Miss?

MALACHY. *(as female adminstrator at NYU)* Yes?

FRANK. Miss. Could I please be admitted to New York university?

MALACHY. Do you have your high school diploma?

FRANK. No. But I read all the writers. I read James Joyce. Oscar Wilde. William Butler Yeats. I read 'em all.

MALACHY. Oh. What a cute brogue. Harriet. Lissena this cute brogue. Say something in brogue for Harriet.

**FRANK.** I want to be assimilated. I want to be the boy next door. I want to have white even teeth. I want to have a name like Chuck. I want to be the man in the grey flannel suit. I want to summer in Southampton. I want to romp in the dunes. I want to caress the golden thighs of an amorous, yielding Presbyterian.

**MALACHY.** He's mine, Harriet. Isn't that the cutest brogue?

**FRANK.** And Harriet said...

**MALACHY.** Yeah.

**FRANK.** And that's how I was admitted to New York University... When I finished there I passed the exam for the teaching license. Then I had to take a speech test.

**MALACHY.** *(speech examiner)* Yes. Yes. Recite something. Preferably, something from the classics.

**FRANK.** Friends. Romans. And countrymen. Lend me your ears. I've come to...

**MALACHY.** What? What? What? What? What is this?

**FRANK.** Shakespeare.

**MALACHY.** I'm aware of that. I'm referring to this... this foreignism.

**FRANK.** I'm not foreign. I'm Irish.

**MALACHY.** Too bad. If you were Caucasian there might be some hope. But this... This brogue will be an impediment to effective pedagogy. I'm afraid you'll have to take a course in remedial speech.

**FRANK.** Remedial speech? Me? Why should I? Weren't two of our own in the White House running the country: John F. Kennedy and his brother, Bobby. Weren't two of our own flourishing in Hollywood - Barry and Ella Fitzgerald? And in New York every two years wasn't one of our own threatening to close down the subways, Mike Quill:

**MALACHY.** *(as Mike Quill)* The mayor of New York, Mr. Lindsley, is too busy meeting the tulip growers of America to meet with the transport workers union of

America. Well, the workers won't wait forever for we will stop the buses from runnin' an' we'll close down them holes in the ground. The people of New York will have to walk but that will be good for their health in general an' their hearts in particular an' they'll see Mr. Lindsley ridin' around in his big limousine. Oh, they will. An' then Mr. Lindsley will haul the transport workers into the court but all I can say is: the judges in their black robes can drop dead.

FRANK. And didn't they understand him? No, I wouldn't take remedial speech. Why should I? Wasn't Irishness erupting everywhere? Everyone singing Irish folk songs, pure and authentic. Everyone wearing white Irish fisherman's sweaters, pure and authentic. How could I cast off this ethnic burden? The answer came with my first teaching job. There were the kids: Black kids, Jewish kids, Chinese kids - and an occasional Irish kid kicked out of Catholic school for thinking. And then it came - that first day, that first class, that first question.

MALACHY. Hey, teach.

FRANK. Yes?

MALACHY. You from Brooklyn or somethin'?

FRANK. Brooklyn! I was assimilated. I am that Yankee Doodle boy!

(sings)

I'M A YANKEE DOODLE DANDEE
YANKEE DOODLE DO OR DIE
YANKEE DOODLE WENT TO LONDON
JUST TO RIDE THE PONIES
I AM THAT YANKEE DOODLE BOY

MALACHY. Excuse me. Is this America?

FRANK. Why, do you have something to say?

MALACHY. I do.

FRANK. Well, don't forget where e'r you roam that you're an Irishman.

MALACHY. That's what I came to forget... It was a lovely sea voyage. Six days of sleeping on a soft white pillow with clean white sheets. Six days of six meals a day - three down and three up. Oh, but what a shock it was to land in New York... The brother, Frank, was gone off in the army, they said. Everything was so fast and noisy. Motor cars and lorries screeching up to red lights and roaring off again when the lights turned green. People rushing from place to place with no time to chat. I went to the old timer.

FRANK. *(as Old Timer)* Kid. Watch out for them.

MALACHY. Who?

FRANK. Never mind. Just watch out for 'em.

MALACHY. He told me of the fierce dangers in the city for the unwary. I was told I'd be hit on the head for being white. Stuck with knives for my money. Cheated in shops for being a greenhorn. Fortified with this wisdom I went out and one of my own got me a job in a hospital.

FRANK. Here. Put on these whites.

MALACHY. White coat. White trousers. Rubber gloves. Bejasus, I'm goin' to be a surgeon.

FRANK. Nah. Dishwasher. Dishes in one end, out the other. Clean.

MALACHY. A miracle. A machine that washes dishes. It's a great country. He didn't say anything about scraping the bones and debris off the plates - and when the machine rattled and clanked and choked to a halt...

FRANK. Hey, what the hell did you do? You broke the goddamn machine. Goddamn Mick. Go back to that miserable country you came from.

MALACHY. You can't talk to me like that, you miserable bollocks.

FRANK. Turn in your whites. You're fired.

MALACHY. Defeated by technology and prejudice I trudged back to my furnished room and my household pets - the cockroaches. I talked to them about my troubles but they weren't listening. *(stamps on one)* Out with me again and didn't one of my own get' me a job in Bloomingdales in the window display department' carrying naked plaster mannequins from the stock room to the windows. As a good Irish Catholic kid it was my first contact with a naked woman. I took a liking to the red-haired one. I called her Sabrina. I took to fondling Sabrina till the head window designer tried to fondle me.

FRANK. Me next, sweetie.

MALACHY. You poxy pervert. I'll give you a thumping.

FRANK. You are fired. You are definitely fired. You are absolutely a beast.

MALACHY. I have a shovel?

FRANK. You're fired.

MALACHY. How would you like to buy a Bible?

FRANK. You're fired.

MALACHY. I have my hook. I'd like to work on the docks.

FRANK. You're not hired.

MALACHY. I went to the old timer. He said:

FRANK. Kid, obviously you don't like to work. Why don't you become an actor?

MALACHY. Off with me to the theatre. Excuse me, sir. I'd like to join your group.

FRANK. *(as producer/director)* Do you have experience?

MALACHY. I don't need any. I'm Irish.

FRANK. Do you have a picture?

MALACHY. I have an autographed picture of the sacred heart of Jesus in my wallet.

FRANK. Here read this.

MALACHY. Ah, a literacy test.

FRANK. Just read it.

MALACHY. "Ten thousand blessings upon all that's here for you've turned me a likely gaffer at the end of all the way I'll go romancin' through a rompin' lifetime from this hour to the dawning of the judgment day."

FRANK. Splendid. You're hired.

MALACHY. I was an actor in an off Broadway play. Great reviews. Then I was invited on the Tonight Show.

FRANK. And here's Malachy.

MALACHY. The Irish said I disgraced them... I was so bad I was asked back... And didn't a man say to me how would you like to open your own bar? And didn't I say yes. Actor, TV personality, saloon keeper. This was America. And the women. I used to think sex was the next number after five but when she said,

FRANK. *(as woman)* Malachy, will you marry me?

MALACHY. I jumped at it ...

*(sings)*

OH, WHISKEY, YOU'RE THE DEVIL
YOU'RE LEADING ME ASTRAY
O'ER THE HILLS AND MOUNTAINS
AND TO AMERIKAY
YOU'RE SWEETER, STRONGER, DACENTER, SPUNKIER NOR
    TAY
OH, WHISKEY YOU'RE ME DARLIN' DRUNK OR SOBER.
I WAS A MARRIED BACHELOR.

FRANK. *(as woman)* And I want a divorce.

MALACHY. Get it from someone else. Everybody loves me. There will be no exceptions. I went to her apartment to explain this to her and after tapping gently on her door - with an oak chair - I was arrested and mana-cled... Oh, if it were only a play. I could have used the quotes from the newspaper: a One-Man St. Patrick's Day Parade with Brass Bands. Forceful... Rowdy. Arresting.

FRANK. *(as Judge)* Malachy McCourt. You are sentenced to six months in prison, sentence suspended.

MALACHY. Strong drink took over. Most people drink to make themselves interesting. I drink to make other people as interesting as myself. I met a man in a bar who asked me if I'd like a job with travel. I found myself in Switzerland, the home of neutrality, secret bank accounts, and cuckoo clocks. The man came to my room lugging a heavy suitcase. *(Man opens suitcase.)* Oh, those are gold bars.

FRANK. *(speaking as if there's no roof to his mouth)* That's right. I want you to take these bars to Bombay.

MALACHY. You want me to smuggle these bars to Bombay?

FRANK. That's right. And when you get to Bombay you call the Mecklai trading company and tell them you're Haaji Khan and they'll tell you what to do.

MALACHY. *(has trouble understanding)* What?

*(FRANK repeats the instructions... slowly.)*

*(MALACHY repeats the instructions.)*

MALACHY. Off to Bombay with me. I called the Mecklai Trading Company.

FRANK. *(Indian)* Hello, Mecklai Trading Company. Can I help you?

MALACHY. This is Haaji Khan.

FRANK. Yes, sir, what can I do for you?

MALACHY. My name is Haaji Khan.

FRANK. Well, how may I assist you?

MALACHY. I was instructed to ring this number and say, "My name is Haaji Khan," and you would tell me what to do.

FRANK. How can I tell you what to do if I don't know the nature of your business?

MALACHY. *(frustrated - speaking with chelf palate)* This is Haaji Khan.

FRANK. Oh, Haaji Khan! Why did you not say so? Did you bring the metal? Then we will send a man to meet you at the Gateway to India at eight o'clock. He will tell you what to do.

MALACHY. Off with me to the Gateway to India, watching the citizenry perambulate.

FRANK. *(in raggedy turban)*

MALACHY. Gunga din.

FRANK. Haaji Khan?

MALACHY. Yeth, Haaji Khan.

FRANK. Walk this way.

MALACHY. I followed him through the slums of Bombay and into a room festooned with multi-colored tapestries. Lolling about on divans were twelve of the most beautiful girls I'd ever seen, gobbling sweetmeats, the girls with red dots on their foreheads. Up the stairs with me to dispose of my golden burden...I returned downstairs to select a bedmate... Come with me, my little parsnip...

I was about to commence proceedings when my eye fell upon a large picture of the sacred heart of Jesus with blood dripping from it, flames erupting and the usual crown of thorns... My ardor diminished. I requested a change of venue which was granted and in another room under a picture of lord Krishna, Irish-Indian relations were cemented forever. Back in New York they gave me a job on the radio - talking. Can you imagine? They paid me to talk. I offended everybody. I was an equal opportunity offender. Hello, you're on the air.

FRANK. You're a disgrace to your poor old Irish mother.

MALACHY. She wouldn't be happy if I weren't. Hello, you're on the air.

FRANK. You're a disgrace to the fair name of Ireland.

MALACHY. Ah, the best of us are. Hello, you're on the air.

FRANK. If you don't like it here why don't you go back where you came from.

MALACHY. Madam, do you know the size of the average womb?

FRANK. (as boss) McCourt, the first amendment doesn't cover this kind of filth.

MALACHY. But this is America.

FRANK. Oh, yeah. Well, you're fired.

MALACHY. Oh, shit.

*(sings)*

I DON'T WORK FOR A LIVING
I GET ALONG ALL RIGHT WITHOUT
I DON'T TOIL ALL DAY
I SUPPOSE IT'S BECAUSE I'M NOT BUILT THAT WAY
SOME PEOPLE WORK FOR LOVE
AND SAY IT'S ALL SUNSHINE AND GAIN
BUT IF I CAN'T GET SUNSHINE
WITHOUT ANY WORK
I THINK I'LL STAY OUT IN THE RAIN.

FRANK. *(as Mother)* Malachy.

MALACHY. Ah, the Irish mother. Over here for a twenty-five year holiday.

FRANK. I have a letter from your father. *(reads)* My dear wife: I take pen in hand to write you this very welcome letter. I have not laid eyes on you in a quarter of a century; a long time to be sure but, measured against eternity, a trifle. I am not the man you knew in bygone days. No longer do I befoul God's air with nicotine fumes and I have not touched drop of strong drink in lo! This many a year.

MALACHY. He hasn't touched a drop since the invention of the funnel.

FRANK. At long last I have found work that is a path to heaven: I am a chef in a monastery. The work is not demanding as the monks spend most of their time fasting and when they feast I slice the bread and pour the water. I have another very important task when the monks die. I have to snip the hair from their nostrils, a necessary job since the nostril hairs of monks sprout at an alarming rate so that sometimes it's a moustache you'd think they have in their coffins. I think of you daily and I pray for our sons. I pray particularly for Frank and Malachy who are endangering their immortal souls by consorting with females of the Presbyterian and Episcopalian persuasion. I know they need the firm hand of a devoted father and I know you need the companionship of a good Catholic husband in a state of grace. Therefore, I have booked passage on a swift ship and will soon be at your side as Mother Church tells us, "What God hath joined let no man put asunder." I will be with you soon so that we can share a bed and a grave. I remain, your fond husband... What should I do, Malachy?

MALACHY. I think you should invite him over, Mam. He sounds like he has a sense of humor. What do you think, Frank?

FRANK. No, Malachy. He deserted us he won't change.

MALACHY. Oh, I think we should give him a chance.

FRANK. All right. We'll give him a chance.

MALACHY. Welcome to America, Dad. Welcome to America... He came off that ship like Toulouse Lautrec... legless drunk and for three weeks he rampaged and roistered till he disappeared into the apartment of two old women next door, alcoholics like himself. My mother asked me to come over and give her a hand to get him out of there. The apartment was strewn with liquor bottles and in the bed there were three bald heads and about six miles of gums. I couldn't figure out which one was my father. I took a chance and shook the one in the middle. It was my father. He sat up. "Malachy, what are you doing here? Who in the name of Jesus are these guys?" Oh, Dad, it was grand to see you arrive in America but it was grander to see you go and so, once more and finally, it was, goodbye, dad.

FRANK. Goodbye, Dad... A few years ago in Belfast we buried him.

MALACHY. We had to. He was dead.

FRANK. Malachy, did you get the tickets for the concert?

MALACHY. Oh, yes. For the Mother's seventieth birthday we took her to an Irish concert at Carnegie hall. We had the worst seats in the house, way up in the Gods.

FRANK. (as Mother) Ooh, God, Malachy, I hope we don't have to go much higher. The emphysema is killing me.

MALACHY. You're going to the top, Mam.

FRANK. *(as Mother)* Ooh, look at that stage. It looks like a postage stamp. I hope we can hear everything.

MALACHY. Don't worry, Mam. Carnegie hall is renowned the world over for the excellence of its acoustics.

FRANK. And my mother said,

BOTH. What?

FRANK. She wanted to see the first moon landing on television. I took her to a bar where my brother Alphie was working. There were a hundred people there. They all wanted to see the moon landing and they wanted to hear Neil Armstrong's first words on the moon. But Alphie said, 'Soon as that capsule lands there will be no more service, no more drink, no more food.' The capsule came down, the hatch opened, Neil Armstrong emerged, put his foot on the moon, opened his mouth to speak - and my mother said:

MALACHY. *(as Mother)* Alphie, could I have a cheeseburger, well done, with a slice of onion on it, please?

FRANK. There are a hundred people walking the world today and if you ask them Neil Armstrong's first words on the moon they'll tell you,

BOTH. Alphie, could I have a cheeseburger, well done, with a slice of onion on it, please?

MALACHY. Not even the emphysema could keep her away from the bingo. One night in a mad dash for her favorite chair she fell, landed in the hospital with a broken hip and there she lingered for three weeks.

FRANK. *(as Mother)* Doctor, take these tubes and needles outta me and stop tormenting me.

MALACHY. *(as Doctor)* No, no, Mrs. McCourt. You could live a long time in a nursing home.

FRANK. *(as Mother)* Doctor, nobody lives in a nursing home.

MALACHY. *(as Doctor)* But you must try to live, at least for the sake of your boys.

FRANK. *(as Mother)* Boys! They're all men now and they'll always be a couple of blaguards. Take these tubes out and let me go.

**FRANK.** *(as self)* Doctor, remove the tubes.

**MALACHY.** If we do that your mother will die.

**FRANK.** Isn't that what she wants?

**MALACHY.** No. No. It's against the state law and medical ethics.

**FRANK.** Don't worry, Doctor. You see...

**BOTH.** We come from a long line of dead people.

**FRANK.** *(sings)*

O LIMERICK IS BEAUTIFUL

**MALACHY.** City of pubs and lowly desires.

**FRANK.**

O GOD BLESS YOU AND KEEP YOU

**MALACHY.** You're a prime candidate for the lust department.

**FRANK.** I had God glued to the roof of my mouth.

**MALACHY.** God knows I wouldn't say a word against the pint.

**FRANK.** Stick with your own.

**MALACHY.** Come to my apartment tonight and I'll explain James Joyce to you.

**FRANK.** *(sings)*

I AM THAT YANKEE DOODLE BOY

**MALACHY.**

SOME PEOPLE WORK FOR LOVE AND SAY IT'S ALL SUNSHINE
AND GAIN

**FRANK.** We come from a long line of...

**BOTH.** *(sing)*

THE BELLS OF HELL
GO TING A LING A LING
FOR YOU BUT NOT FOR ME
OH, DEATH WHERE IS THY STING A LING A LING
OR GRAVE THY VICTORY
IF YOU MEET THE UNDERTAKER
OR THE YOUNG MAN FROM THE PRU
HAVE A PINT WITH WHAT'S LEFT OVER
AND I'LL SAY GOODNIGHT TO YOU

**BOTH.** *(sing)*
       FOR THE BELLS OF HELL GO TING A LING A LING
       FOR YOU BUT NOT FOR ME
       OH, DEATH WHERE IS THY STING A LING A LING
       OR GRAVE THY VICTORY

**The End**